T5-CQB-126

Just Your Cup of TEA

by Kathie Janger

THE AMERICAN ★COOKING★ GUILD™

Boynton Beach, Florida

Dedication
Many thanks to Karen and Dan Perrino and to my family for their support and enthusism. Special appreciation goes to the Tea Council of the U.S.A., Inc., the Tea Association of the U.S.A., Inc., and to all my tea and treat tasters.

—Edited by Rena Neff
—Cover Photograph by Burwell & Burwell
—Illustrations by Jim Haynes
—Cover Design and Layout by Pearl & Associates, Inc.

Revised Edition 1997
Copyright © 1995 by Kathie Janger.
All rights reserved.
Printed in U.S.A.
ISBN 0-942320-50-6

More...Quick Recipes for Creative Cooking!
The American Cooking Guild's *Collector's Series* includes over 30 popular cooking topics such as Barbeque, Breakfast & Brunches, Chicken, Cookies, Hors d' Oeuvres, Seafood, Tea, Coffee, Pasta, Pizza, Salads, Italian and many more. Each book contains more than 50 selected recipes. For a catalog of these and many other full sized cookbooks, send $1 to the address below and a coupon will be included for $1 off your first order.

Cookbooks Make Great Premiums!
The American Cooking Guild has been the premier publisher of private label and custom cookbooks since 1981. Retailers, manufacturers, and food companies have all chosen The American Cooking Guild to publish their premium and promotional cookbooks. For further information on our special markets programs please contact the address.

The American Cooking Guild
3600-K South Congress Avenue
Boynton Beach, FL 33426

Contents

Introduction

Beverages

Finger Foods

Sweets

More About Tea

Introduction

You were probably just a toddler the first time you sat down to tea. The plastic teapot and wobbly cups may have been empty, but you poured and sipped with unbridled delight. Imagine getting in touch with that feeling again, actually interrupting your life's routine to establish a new, cherished pastime, a stop-the-world-and-smell-the-jasmine interlude.

The whole idea of taking tea is related to quality of life. People in a household that gathers for tea are making time for each other. Businesses in other countries that mandate a mid-afternoon break, when a tea cart stops at each desk and dispenses free refreshments, are taking time to value and respect their employees. These are pauses that satisfy and rejuvenate and keep us in touch with each other. Taking tea is more than a few leaves and some boiling water; taking tea is a kind of fitness for the soul.

So let's get started. You might want a little background information and maybe a few guidelines, but making tea is fast and easy. The recipes for beverages in the following pages are made with loose tea. You can, of course, substitute tea bags (there's about one teaspoon of tea in a standard sachet), but doing so will limit quality, flavor and variety—not to mention the opportunity for tea leaf reading. Join the fun. After your perusal, perhaps you'll agree: if you're tea-less, you are deprived!

The History of Tea

The first written record of tea dates back to China in the fourth century, where the upper class and priests enjoyed it long before it became available to the masses. Later, tea became a commercial commodity, and by the eighth century the cultivation of tea had spread to Japan. In the twelfth century, *Cha-no-yu*, or the way of tea, originated in Japan. Known as the Japanese Tea Ceremony, it is a ritual designed to foster tranquility and humility.

The Dutch brought tea to Europe from Asia, and they controlled tea commerce for some time. Finally, however, the British East India Trading Company took command of the tea trade, at which point the beverage became widely available. Coffee houses began offering tea, and its popularity soon outpaced that of coffee.

Many battles have been waged in the name of tea. The Boston Tea Party in 1773 is one that grew out of the tea tax that was imposed in Britain and also levied on the colonists in America. Eleven years later, Americans sailed under their own flag to China, where they loaded a cargo of tea.

The United States is the second largest importer of tea in the world, the first being Great Britain. The tea bag and iced tea were both American inventions. Thomas Sullivan who was a New York tea merchant, is given credit for the tea bag and the first iced tea was served at the 1904 Louisiana Purchase Exposition in St. Louis, Missouri.

More than three-fourths of the tea consumed in the United States is served cold. Shelves in supermarkets abound with a wide variety of prepared tea beverages in the refrigerated and soft drink aisles and in vending machines. Tea is also grown in this country. After a century of effort, there is now a functioning tea estate in Charleston, South Carolina. And, believe it or not, a board of tea tasters still acts to determine the acceptability of imported teas before they are distributed in the United States.

How to Hold a Tea-Tasting

Visit your specialty tea dealer. Decide on the assortment of teas you will offer your guests. Your tea dealer might be willing to conduct the tea tasting for you. If that offer is made, accept it but suggest a conservative selection of teas unless your guests are true aficionados.

Make a list of the teas, noting their trade names, classes (black tea, green tea and so on), grades, where they are grown and the styles in which they are usually served in their native habitats. Include interesting tidbits of lore such as the fact that the herbal tea you have selected was once used to combat stomachaches. Add a column to your sheet for guests' comments.

The following are suggested guidelines. Your personal style and ideas are sure to enhance the unique event you host.

Have ready:

1. A copy of the list of teas you prepared for each guest.

2. Six different kinds of loose tea and loose tea blends: one black, one green, one blend, one herbal, one blossom-scented and one blended with spices.

3. Several tea kettles or a tea urn. You'll need a good supply of boiling water, and you won't want to spend all your time resetting the kettle to boil.

4. One teapot for each tea. Try matching the tea to the teapot. Use an Asian-style teapot for green tea, and so on.

5. Six cups per guest, one for each kind of tea. You may need to borrow to get enough cups and a variety of styles. Use tea glasses, demitasse cups and Chinese cups without handles, for example.

6. Spoons, milk, sugar or honey and sliced lemon. Encourage your guests to taste the tea plain, but be prepared for such requests.

7. Use your dining room table for the array, or set up tea-tasting stations on several smaller tables. Use cloth table linens and napkins to set the mood. You may want to choose a cloth printed with roses if one of your teas is a Rose Pouchong, or select a batik print for a Ceylon tea.

8. Serve simple finger sandwiches and sweets, but keep the focus on the tea.

9. Brew one tea at a time, and encourage your guests to watch when the boiling water hits the tea, because some tea leaves put on quite a show. Pour only a taste. You can always brew more of a particular tea later. Discuss characteristics such as aroma and color and the origin of each tea. Have guests jot down their opinions in the remarks column of the list you distributed. Don't take criticisms personally.

10. Have a good time. Let your guests take turns brewing and serving the teas so everyone participates. If there is wild enthusiasm for the occasion, suggest forming a once-a-month tea-tasting club. Remind guests to take their evaluation lists home to help with future tea-buying expeditions.

Tea-Pouring Etiquette

1. Scald the teapot with boiling water, swirl it around and empty the water into a waste bowl.

2. Measure tea leaves into the teapot. Use one teaspoon of leaves per cup of water.

3. Pour in freshly drawn boiling water, stir and replace lid.

4. Optional: place a tea cozy over the teapot.

5. Steep 3 to 5 minutes depending upon the kind of tea you have selected and upon your taste. When the time has elapsed, stir the pot again.

6. Scald the individual teacups (this is optional).

7. Strain all the tea into another scalded teapot (this is optional).

8. It is an honor to be asked to pour tea, so make that offer to one of your guests if you like.

9. If you are pouring, strain the first cup for your guest of honor.

10. Inquire if the guest would like hot water added (to dilute the brew), milk, lemon or sweetener. Pass that cup to the guest, and discard the strained tea leaves into the waste bowl. Continue the pouring.

11. Offer refreshments to your guests using small plates, cloth napkins and utensils as appropriate to the menu. If you are clustered around a table, the platters can be passed. If you are serving a large cake or a trifle, guests can pass their plates to you for a helping.

12. Discard any leftover tea into the waste bowl. Brew a fresh batch for subsequent pouring.

Tea Party Menus

Lazy Sunday
Coddled Eggs
Cucumber Tea Sandwiches
Rosy Ham Spread
Currant Scones with butter and jam
Banana Pecan Muffins
Lemon Thins
Tea
Lemon, sugar, milk

Pre-Theatre
Meat Pasties
Egg Salad Triangles
Rarebit Treats
Watercress Pinwheels
Buttered Roquefort Canapes
Strawberry Banana Trifle
Tea
Lemon, sugar, milk

Bridal Shower
Smoked Salmon Canapes
Cheese Straws
Olive Pimiento Bites
Egg Salad Triangles
Cashew Coconut Meringues
Pecan Shortbread
Orange Spice Tea Cake
Pineapple Tea Loaf
Berry Lime Tarts
Assortment of Teas
Lemon, sugar, milk

Saturday Patio Party
Rosy Ham Spread
Radish Tea Sandwiches
Cucumber Tea Sandwiches
Cheddary Cheese Snaps
Curried Chutney Spread
Almond Wafers
15-Minute Tea Cakes
Solar Tea
Spa Cooler

Brewing and Serving Tea

Teakettles

You can boil water in a saucepan, in a hot pot at a college dorm or over a campfire. But whether stove-top or electric, whistling or automatic shut-off, a teakettle is the most necessary and practical piece of equipment for brewing tea. Teakettles come in enamel-finish, glass, stainless steel and so on. A good teakettle has a lid that fits securely, with either a lip or a safety chain to keep the lid in place. Check the capacity of the teakettle to see if it will accommodate your needs. Test it for weight and ease of use. Whatever kettle you acquire, keep it clean. (Have you looked inside your teakettle lately?) Fill it with fresh water before each use as water quality is of primary importance in making tea.

Tea Urns

A large, ornamental container with a lid and a faucet and usually its own heating device, a tea urn is designed to hold a sizable quantity of hot water for the purpose of serving tea to large groups of people. It may be of fancy design in gleaming silver, and have either a pedestal or footed base.

Teapots

Teapots are made in a range of materials such as bone china, pottery and silver. There are a myriad of shapes and styles from elegant to whimsical. Teapots come in tea-for-one as well as company's-coming sizes. A good teapot features a handle that is designed to keep your knuckles from being singed on the hot bowl of the teapot. The lid should have a security lip so that it doesn't suddenly fall off while you're pouring. The lid should also have a strategic airhole in it that allows the tea to pour through the spout smoothly and easily. And, very important, a teapot should inspire your fancy and capture your imagination or even transport you back in time. A teapot can become a romantic possession that stands ready to help you celebrate, remember and relax.

Infusers

Infusers usually are made of stainless steel. These hinged, perforated utensils feature a compartment for holding tea leaves. The tea leaves are measured into the infuser, which is then closed and placed into the teapot or teacup with boiling water. The tea is allowed to brew, and then the infuser is removed to prevent overbrewing of the tea. Some infusers look like a spoon with a lid while others are ball-shaped with a chain attached for ease of removing them from the pot. Tea balls come in various sizes. Make sure to use one that is large enough, because tea leaves expand dramatically during brewing.

Strainers

Strainers are, indeed, the stuff of which collections are made. Fabricated of stainless steel, wire mesh, silver or bamboo in styles from the ornate to the ordinary, strainers can be as simple as a small sieve or a bamboo basket. Other styles are richly decorative, but all feature at least one handle and a perforated bowl that is designed to catch tea leaves after brewing. They are placed atop an individual teacup and the brewed tea is poured through. There is one kind of strainer that attaches with prongs into the spout of a teapot.

A mote spoon is a utensil with a perforated bowl that is used to remove, from a poured cup, tea leaves that have escaped initial straining. You might want to use mote spoons in place of ordinary teaspoons.

Lemon Juicers

Used at teatime, juicers corral the seeds and pulp so that only the juice from wedges of lemon or orange is deposited into the brewed tea. While knotting half a lemon in cheesecloth would suffice to strain the unwanted bits, a juicer makes the squeezing easier and contributes to the overall decor and elegance of your tea tray.

Tea Caddies

Tea has been stored and sold in tea caddies for thousands of years. The word caddy has its origin in the word *kati*, which is a Malay weight measure (about 1.12 pounds). Basically a storage tin or a box of fine wood, they were sometimes decorated with inlaid designs and usually featured a locking mechanism to protect the revered tea. An early tea caddy held about one pound of tea and was as prized as its contents were valued.

With the exception of that in specialty shops, most of the tea on retailers' shelves today, however, is packaged in foil or cellophane. Because tea is vulnerable to absorbing odors and flavors of other foods it is stored near, it is recommended that you place your tea in canisters or airtight containers immediately after purchase.

Tea Cozies

Tea cozies are insulated cloth covers for teapots that are designed to keep tea warm while it brews. Because their use intensifies the heat within the teapot, use them only for the few minutes the tea is steeped in the teapot, or don't use one at all. Tea that has already been brewed but not served is not kept warm for additional pourings. Instead, a fresh pot is brewed and enjoyed.

Sugar Tongs

If you're eager to implement the phrase, "One lump, or two," you must have lump sugar and sugar tongs—a sugar shell simply won't do. Acquire one to match your silver pattern, or haunt antique establishments to find one with a fine patina or a repousse style. Once your focus is narrowed on this charming utensil, look out: It will be hard to choose just one. Rationalize a multiple acquisition by vowing to use sugar tongs to serve olives, pickles, bonbons or small savories.

Tea Sets

Tea sets can be heirlooms or simply a random collection of tea brewing and serving equipment. The traditional tea set includes a large tray, a teapot, an extra pot or tea kettle for additional hot water (or a kettle), a waste bowl, a sugar bowl and a small milk pitcher. Coffeepots are not part of a formal tea set.

Accessories like infusers, strainers, squeezers and sugar tongs are usually acquired separately from a teaset. The tray and teapot are self-explanatory. The water in the extra pot or kettle is used to dilute brewed tea or to brew the next pot of tea. A waste bowl is handy for depositing used tea leaves that are left in the strainer, small amounts of leftover brewed tea, squeezed wedges of lemon or the pot-scalding water that has warmed the teapot. In short, a waste bowl collects the refuse at teatime.

Teacups

You may already have all the teacups you need, but if you're planning a new acquisition consider the following. Examine the handle of the cup. Try holding it for balance. Does it afford you a secure grip? Will it do the same when the cup is full of hot tea? Do your lower fingers tend to rest against the bowl of the cup? If the bowl of the cup has a slight pedestal at the bottom, you might be spared a scorched finger or two. Does the cup fit snugly into the saucer without rocking? Is the saucer large enough to accommodate a teaspoon resting alongside the cup?

In colonial America, the first known teacups were really just bowls, crude earthenware containers with no handles. Indeed, some early tea caddies had a special compartment for the tea bowl and another section for the loose tea. It might be inferred that this was the earliest form of a tea set. Teacups without handles are used today in Chinese and Japanese restaurants or in those countries themselves. Yet, when we think of drinking hot tea, most of us picture a graceful and delicate bone china teacup. Some might prefer a matched set; others might build an assortment around a grandmother's treasured cup. Others might find pleasure in collecting teacups when they travel. Such an array will spark special interest, fond memories and conversation over tea.

You might be in the habit of using an insulated, spill-proof container that accompanies you on the way to work, or it might be your practice to make do with a Styrofoam cup from a carryout. Perhaps you get a little cranky when your favorite chipped mug—the one that holds exactly the right quantity of tea and keeps it exactly the right temperature—becomes the site of a seed-sprouting experiment. Whatever the vessel from which you sip the heady brew, that which matters is what matters to you.

Tea Glasses

In some countries, no one would think of drinking tea from a teacup. In the former Soviet Union, Morocco or Turkey, for instance, tea—hot, strong and sweet—is served in a glass. Street vendors dispensing tea do a brisk trade, and runners deliver trays of tea to shopkeepers' customers. Tea glasses are usually plain and cylindrically shaped, similar to a standard bar glass. Fancier versions come with a metal filigree "sleeve" with a handle, into which the glass is nestled. A spoon is plopped into the glass, then sugar and hot tea are added. Contrary to western etiquette, the spoon remains in the glass while the tea is drunk.

Serving Pieces and Utensils

There is no end to the available choices for serving pieces. They come in silver, crystal, porcelain, earthenware and china. Some are pierced, scalloped or filigree styles while others are etched or rimmed in gold and silver. There are even traditional geometric, basket and fish shapes. You can certainly serve a proper tea with the plates and bowls you have on hand, but such accessories as a crystal trifle dish, biscuit barrel, honey pot, a toast rack, a sugar basin, a cake plate with pedestal base, a compotier (fruit dish) and a handled hostess or tiered tidbit tray certainly help create a special mood at tea time.

Caddy spoons for measuring tea leaves, pastry serving tongs, cake breakers, berry spoons, condiment ladles, mote spoons and lemon forks are only a few special utensils that add dimension and tradition to your tea tray. Somehow, the simple fact of owning these pieces is a personal statement of dedication to the decorum and refinement of teatime ritual.

Have your third-grader make you a ceramic lemon-wedge dish in art class, browse in your local china department or gift shop, pore over catalogs, become a regular at yard sales or consignment shops and forage in the attic or the basement for unusual serving pieces and utensils that reflect your individual style and that will forever be labeled as your "tea things."

Linens

Use *cloth* tablecloths and napkins if you want to achieve an atmosphere of quality. Fine damask or linen, cheerful or quaint cotton prints or even easy-care fabrics are acceptable.

Don't use plastic or paper. There are standards to observe when you serve afternoon tea. This is an event of culture and class.

Beverages

SOLAR TEA

Hot Tea

Try adding whole cloves, mint leaves, slivers of fresh, peeled ginger or cardamom pods to the teapot with the tea leaves before brewing.

4 (6 ounce) cups water
4 teaspoons black tea leaves
Sweetener
Milk
Lemon

Fill a clean kettle with freshly drawn cold water and bring to a bubbling boil. To warm the teapot, scald it with boiling water, swish it around, and discard the water. Measure tea leaves into teapot and add boiling water; stir and replace lid.

(Optional: cover teapot with a tea cozy. Steep for 3 to 5 minutes.) If desired, you can also scald the teacups prior to filling. Stir again, and strain into tea cups, or strain all the tea into another scalded teapot. Serve with the sweetener of your choice and milk or a squeeze of lemon.

Note: Use of a tea cozy may reduce the steeping time. Never reuse tea leaves. Try to decant all the brewed tea. If any remains, throw it out and make a fresh pot for refills.

Yield: About 4 servings

Iced Tea

Use a blend of two or three kinds of tea and spice with cloves or cinnamon or both.

4 cups (32 ounces) freshly drawn cool water
10 teaspoons tea leaves
Mint leaves
Lemon or orange wedges
Sweetener

Place 16 ounces of the water in a pitcher; set aside. Place tea leaves in a four-cup measure and add 16 ounces of boiling water. Allow to steep for 5 minutes.

Strain the brewed tea into the pitcher and stir. Serve over cubed ice in individual tall glasses. Garnish with a sprig of mint, lemon or orange wedges. Sweeten as desired.

Yield: About 6 servings

Spiced Apple Tea

You can adjust the sweetness of this drink to taste.

2 cups apple juice
¼ cup granulated sugar
6 whole cloves
2 three-inch pieces cinnamon bark
1 teaspoon ground nutmeg
6 teaspoons tea leaves
6 (6 ounce) cups boiling water
Additional sweetener if desired

In a saucepan on medium heat, combine the apple juice and sugar.
In a square of cheesecloth, place the cloves, cinnamon bark and nutmeg. Tie shut and add to apple juice mixture. Bring to a boil and simmer 5 to 10 minutes. Remove cheesecloth.
Measure tea leaves into teapot; add boiling water and steep 5 minutes.
Strain tea into a heat-proof carafe and add juice mixture. Serve hot.
Yield: 8 servings

Tucson Tea

Garnish this delicious beverage with lime and mint and sweeten as desired.

4 teaspoons tea leaves
4 (6 ounce) cups water
1 cup apricot nectar
½ cup orange juice
Lime wedges
Mint leaves
Sweetener

Place tea leaves in a scalded teapot. Pour in boiling water and steep for 5 minutes.
Strain tea into a heat-proof pitcher, add apricot nectar and orange juice. Chill. Stir occasionally.
To serve, stir well and pour into tall glasses over ice.
Yield: About 5 servings

Solar Tea

Serve over ice in tall glasses. Sweeten as desired and garnish with lemon and orange wedges.

8 teaspoons tea leaves
1 Tablespoon mint leaves
8 (6 ounce) cups freshly drawn cold water
Lemon wedges
Orange wedges
Sweetener

Place tea and mint in a stainless steel infuser. Drop infuser into a large glass jug. Add water and cover.

Place jug in the hot sun for 2 hours (depending upon the heat of the day, it may take less time).

Remove infuser and serve tea over ice.

Yield: About ½ gallon

Spa Cooler

Pour over ice in tall glasses. Add a squeeze of lime and a straw. Garnish with skewers of pineapple, strawberries and orange chunks.

4 teaspoons tea leaves
4 (6 ounce) cups water
1 pint (16 ounces) cranberry juice
1 three-inch piece cinnamon bark
2 Tablespoons seedless raspberry syrup
8 ounces soda water
Sweetener, to taste
Lime wedges
Fresh pineapple chunks
Strawberries
Fresh orange chunks

In a warmed teapot, place tea leaves; add boiling water and steep 5 minutes.

Strain tea into a pitcher, drop in cinnamon bark, add syrup and cool.

Add cranberry juice and mix, then chill. Just before serving, add soda water and stir. Adjust sweetness to taste.

Yield: 5 to 6 servings

Chinese Tea

Serve this tea in small pottery cups without handles. Sweeten as desired.

2 teaspoons black Keemun tea leaves
2 teaspoons green Lung Ching tea leaves
4 (6 ounce) cups water
Sweetener

Place tea leaves in a warmed teapot. Pour in boiling water, and steep for 3 to 5 minutes.
Yield: 4 to 6 servings

Indian Tea

For a stronger infusion of spices, place them in one cup of the water and simmer for 15 to 30 minutes, then pour mixture into a warmed teapot and brew tea leaves as directed.

4-5 teaspoons Assam tea leaves
4 small pods of cardamom
4 whole cloves
1 piece cinnamon bark, about one-inch long
4 (6 ounce) cups water
Hot milk
Brown sugar or honey

Place tea leaves, cardamom, cloves and cinnamon bark in a warmed teapot. Pour in boiling water and steep 5 minutes.

Strain into teacups. Serve with hot milk and sweeten with brown sugar or honey.
Yield: 4 to 5 servings

Chamomile Tisane

Feel free to sweeten this wonderful infusion to taste.

4 teaspoons dried chamomile
4 (6 ounce) cups boiling water
Sugar or other sweetener, to taste

Make a decoction by combining chamomile and water in a glass, stainless steel or enameled saucepan.
Boil for 5 minutes, then strain into individual cups.
Yield: 4 servings

Russian Tea

Serve over cracked ice in tall glasses. Garnish with slices of lemon and orange.

6 teaspoons tea leaves
2 whole cloves
2 whole allspice
4 (6 ounce) cups boiling water
½ cup orange juice
Lemon wedges for squeezing
Sugar or sweetener, to taste

In a large tea ball infuser, combine tea, cloves and allspice. Put infuser in warmed teapot, add boiling water and orange juice. Brew 5 to 6 minutes. Remove infuser.
Serve in heat-proof glasses, adding a squeeze of lemon juice. Sweeten to taste.
Yield: 4 servings

Cloudy Iced Tea

Hard water can cause cloudiness. Try using bottled water for iced tea. Or, store freshly brewed tea at room temperature if you plan to use it all the same day. To clear cloudy tea, add ½ cup of freshly boiled water to refrigerated tea.

Thai Iced Tea

Sip this very sweet concoction through a straw. If you don't stir it, the drink will have a variegated rust color.

6 teaspoons Thai or South China red leaf tea leaves
4 (6 ounce) cups water
Condensed milk

Place tea (this variety has a powdery consistency) in a coffee filter to brew. Pour boiling water through and drain into a warmed teapot.

To serve, fill stemmed goblets with crushed ice and add hot tea till about two-thirds full.

Fill glasses with condensed milk and serve.

Note: for a non-sweet drink, you can use evaporated milk in place of the condensed milk.

Yield: 4 to 5 servings

Hot Tea Toddy

After you strain the tea into a mug, garnish with a cinnamon stick and add more sweetener if desired.

½ teaspoon unsalted butter
1 teaspoon brown sugar
1 Tablespoon rum or ½ teaspoon rum flavoring
1½ teaspoons tea leaves
8 ounces boiling water
1 whole clove
1 three-inch piece cinnamon bark
Sweetener, if desired

In an earthenware mug, combine butter, brown sugar and rum.

Place tea leaves, clove and cinnamon bark in a one-cup measure.

Add boiling water; steep 5 minutes. Stir well, strain into the mug and serve hot.

Yield: 1 serving

Herbal Refresher

Sweeten this fruity tea to taste and garnish with whole fresh mint leaves.

4 (6 ounce) cups water
2 Tablespoons red raspberry tea leaves
2 Tablespoons blueberry tea leaves
4 whole cloves
Sweetener
Fresh mint leaves

Make a decoction in an enameled or stainless steel saucepan by combining water, herbs and cloves. Bring to a bubbling boil. Reduce heat and simmer 5 to 10 minutes.

Strain into a scalded teapot.

Yield: 4 servings

Cold Water Tea

6 teaspoons tea leaves
4 cups (32 ounces) cold water
Sweetener, to taste
Lemon wedges, as garnish

Measure tea leaves into a pitcher or jug. Add freshly drawn cold water and refrigerate overnight.

Strain into another pitcher to remove leaves. Serve over ice with sweetener and lemon, or use in other cold tea recipes.

Yield: 1 quart

Tea and Aluminum

Avoid brewing tea in aluminum pots or saucepans. A chemical reaction can occur that causes the tea to turn black.

Sangria Fiestea

Serve this at your next party instead of beer or wine.

5 (6 ounces) cups water
3 Tablespoons sugar
4 teaspoons tea leaves
2 cups red wine
1 cup orange juice
1 cup white grape juice
1 cup fresh fruit (peaches, oranges, apples, melon), cubed
1 pint (16 ounces) soda water

In a small saucepan, combine 1 cup of the water and all the sugar. Bring to a boil and simmer 5 minutes; set aside.

Using the cold water brewing method (page 22), brew tea in remaining water.

In a large pitcher or jug, place sugar syrup, brewed tea, wine, juices and fruit. Chill.

Just before serving, add soda water to pitcher and stir well. Serve in stemmed glasses, spooning some of the fruit into each glass.

Yield: 8 to 10 servings

Fruity Tea Punch

If desired, add ¾ cup rum to the punchbowl before serving.

½ cup granulated sugar
½ teaspoon whole allspice
6 teaspoons tea leaves
6 (6 ounce) cups water
1 cup orange juice
1 cup apple juice
1 package (10 ounces) frozen strawberries and juice, defrosted
1 quart (32 ounces) ginger ale

In a large saucepan, combine sugar, allspice and 1 cup of the water. Boil 5 minutes; set aside.

Using the last 5 cups of water, brew tea leaves, steep 5 minutes and strain into sugar syrup. Add orange and apple juices and mix. Adjust sweetness to taste. Chill overnight.

Just before serving, add strawberries with their juice and the ginger ale. Pour into a punch bowl, add ice and serve in punch cups.

Yield: 12 to 15 servings

Finger Foods

Cucumber Tea Sandwiches

Use a seedless cucumber for the best-tasting canapes.

> *1 three-ounce package cream cheese, softened*
> *½ teaspoon garlic salt*
> *1 teaspoon chopped chives*
> *½ teaspoon chervil*
> *½ cucumber, peeled*
> *8 slices white bread*
> *Dill weed, for garnish*

In a small bowl, combine cream cheese, salt, chives and chervil. Mix well and refrigerate at least 2 hours.

To assemble, cut 8 slices of cucumber; set aside. Using a large biscuit or cookie cutter, cut a round from each slice of bread.

Spread bread with cream cheese mixture and top with a cucumber slice.

Garnish each open-faced sandwich with a sprinkle of dill weed.

Yield: 8 canapes

Watercress Pinwheels

Freeze any remaining bread, or spread with alternate fillings to make other flavors of pinwheel sandwiches.

> *4 Tablespoons watercress*
> *1 three-ounce package cream cheese, softened*
> *2 Tablespoons mayonnaise*
> *salt to taste*
> *1 whole loaf white bread, unsliced*

Wash watercress and pat dry with paper towel. Pluck leaves from stems and mince the leaves.

In a small bowl, combine watercress, cream cheese, mayonnaise and salt. Mix well. Refrigerate for at least 2 hours.

Remove crusts from all sides of bread loaf. Cut bread lengthwise into four long slices. Spread with filling, then roll up the long side of the bread like a jelly roll; chill. When cold, cut ¼" slices from the roll with a sharp knife to create pinwheels.

Ribbon Sandwiches: Use all four slabs of bread and spread each with a different filling such as pimiento cheese, radish or ham spread. To help the tiers stick together, spread the underside of the second and third slices with unsalted butter or mayonnaise. Stack bread slices on top of one another, press layers firmly together, and chill. When cold, slice through all the tiers to make colorful ribbon sandwiches.

Yield: 6-8 canapes per slab of bread

Olive Pimiento Bites

Trying using this as a spread when making radish or cucumber sandwiches.

2 stalks celery
6 pimiento-stuffed green olives
3 Tablespoons chopped pimiento
1 three-ounce package cream cheese, softened
1 Tablespoon mayonnaise
Paprika for garnish

Clean celery and cut stalks in 1-inch pieces; set aside.

Chop olives fine and place in a small bowl. Add pimiento, cream cheese and mayonnaise; mix well.

Stuff each celery piece with the cream cheese mixture; dust with paprika. Arrange on a small plate or use as a garnish on a platter of assorted canapes.

Yield: 12 to 15 pieces

Egg Salad Triangles

If you prefer, omit the top layer of bread and garnish with crisp bacon.

2 eggs, hard-cooked
2 small scallions, minced
3 Tablespoons mayonnaise
Salt and pepper
8 slices whole wheat bread

Chop eggs fine. Mince scallions (including some of the green top). Place egg and scallions in a small bowl. Add mayonnaise, salt and pepper; mix well. Taste for seasoning. Add more mayonnaise to taste.

Refrigerate for several hours. Remove crusts from bread. Spread 4 slices with egg salad, top with remaining slices. Cut the sandwiches diagonally before serving.

Yield: 8 pieces

Radish Tea Sandwiches

If you like radishes, these are as delicious as they are pretty.

8 fresh red radishes
2 Tablespoons butter, softened
4 slices fresh white bread
Dill weed, for garnish
Salt and pepper, for garnish

Wash radishes and pat dry. Cut into very thin circles.

Cut crusts from bread, then cut the slices in half to make a total of eight rectangles.

Butter the bread generously, and top each piece with several slices of radish, slightly overlapping. Sprinkle with dill, salt and pepper.

Yield: 8 tea sandwiches

Rarebit Treats

Cut sliced packaged Cheddar cheese into quarters to yield cheese squares of about the right size. Watch these canapes closely as they broil because the cheese browns quickly.

12 slices cocktail-sized pumpernickel bread
2 Tablespoons mustard
2 slices bacon, cooked and cut into 1-inch pieces
12 thin slices Cheddar cheese, each 1¾" square
4 cherry tomatoes

In a toaster oven or broiler, very lightly toast the bread. Spread each slice with mustard and top with a piece of cooked bacon.

Cover bacon with a square of cheese.

Cut each cherry tomato into 3 slices; place one slice on top of each canape. Broil to melt cheese. Serve warm.

Yield: 12 canapes

Buttered Roquefort Canapes

If you prefer, substitute any blue-veined cheese for the Roquefort.

1 three-ounce package cream cheese, softened
1 Tablespoon crumbled Roquefort cheese
1 teaspoon minced onion
1 Tablespoon butter, softened
Worcestershire sauce, to taste
8 slices French bread
3 cherry tomatoes, thinly sliced
Black pepper, for garnish

In a small bowl, combine cream cheese, Roquefort, onion, butter and Worcestershire sauce. Mix well. Refrigerate at least 2 hours.

Spread cheese mixture on rounds of French bread; garnish each canape with a slice of tomato and a grating of fresh black pepper.

Yield: 8 canapes

Smoked Salmon Canapes

For onion lovers, combine butter and capers and spread on bread. Top with a thin slice of onion, then continue as directed.

3 ounces smoked salmon
2 Tablespoons butter or cream cheese, softened
2 Tablespoons onion, minced
1 Tablespoon capers, minced
8 slices cocktail-sized pumpernickel bread
1 egg, hard-cooked and sliced into circles
Dill weed, for garnish

Cut smoked salmon into eight squares; set aside.

In a small bowl, combine the butter or cream cheese, onion and capers.

Spread the bread slices with the butter or cream cheese mixture. Top each piece with a square of smoked salmon and a slice of egg.

Garnish each canape with a sprinkle of dill weed.

Yield: 8 canapes

Cheese Straws

Serve these delicate treats in a pretty napkin-lined basket or in a decorative small vase. Store any leftovers in an air-tight container or freeze.

> *1⅓ cups all-purpose flour*
> *⅔ cup grated Parmesan cheese*
> *1 teaspoon salt*
> *⅔ cup shortening*
> *6 Tablespoons cold water*
> *Additional Parmesan for rolling dough*
> *Paprika for rolling dough*

In a medium bowl, sift together flour, cheese and salt. Cut in shortening with a pastry blender until mixture looks like cornmeal. Add water and mix quickly. (If needed, add more water a tablespoon at a time until dough can be gathered into a ball.)

"Flour" the rolling surface with Parmesan and paprika. Roll dough to ½ inch; lift dough, dust surface with more cheese and paprika.

Flip dough over and roll to ⅛ inch thickness.

Cut dough into strips, each ¼ inch wide and about 4 inches long. Twist each strip, then place on a cookie sheet.

Bake at 400° for 7 to 9 minutes.

Note: If you prefer, you can use half butter and half shortening.

Yield: About 72 four-inch straws

Cheddary Cheese Snaps

Serve these warm for the best flavor. They store well in an airtight container, or they can be frozen for future use.

> *3 ounces grated cheddar cheese*
> *3 Tablespoons butter or margarine*
> *½ teaspoon Worcestershire sauce*
> *7 Tablespoons all-purpose flour*
> *6 pimiento-stuffed olives, chopped*

In a medium bowl, combine the cheese, butter or margarine, Worcestershire sauce and flour; mix well. Add chopped olives and mix.

Roll into 12 balls and place on ungreased cookie sheet. Refrigerate the cookie sheet for an hour.

Bake at 400° for 8 to 10 minutes.

Yield: 12 pieces

Curried Chutney Spread

If you don't like mango, use any fruit chutney of your choice.

1 Tablespoon butter
⅓ cup chopped almonds
1 package (3 ounces) cream cheese, softened
¼ teaspoon curry powder
2 Tablespoons mango chutney
Wheat crackers

In a small pan over medium heat, melt the butter and lightly brown the almonds; set aside.

In a small bowl, combine the cream cheese, curry powder and chutney. Add almonds and mix well.

Refrigerate for at least 2 hours. Serve with crackers.

Yield: about ¾ cup

Pimiento Cheese Spread

You can make open-faced canapes or traditional luncheon sandwiches with this delicious mixture.

1 cup grated cheddar cheese
1 Tablespoon onion, minced
2 Tablespoons sweet pickle relish
1 small (2 ounce) jar chopped pimiento
2 Tablespoons mayonnaise, or to taste
Salt, to taste
1 cocktail-sized loaf rye bread

In a small mixing bowl, combine cheese, onion, relish and pimiento. Add enough mayonnaise to hold mixture together. Add salt to taste. Refrigerate for at least 2 hours. Spread on slices of cocktail rye bread.

Yield: About 1 cup

Rosy Ham Spread

Spread mixture on bread slices and garnish with pimiento, or serve on crackers or mini bagel halves.

4 thin slices of boiled ham
2 Tablespoons finely chopped celery
1 Tablespoon minced onion
1 Tablespoon sweet pickle relish
2 Tablespoons mayonnaise
8 slices cocktail-sized rye bread
Pimiento strips, for garnish

Mince or grind the ham and place in a small bowl. Add celery, onion, relish and mayonnaise. Mix well.

Refrigerate at least 2 hours before spreading on bread.

Garnish each canape with a strip of pimiento.

Yield: 8 canapes

Keeping Tea Sandwiches Fresh

Arrange sandwiches on a serving platter. Dampen a tea towel or cloth napkin and cover the platter.

Meat Pasties

Serve these savory meat pies warm for the best flavor.

Dough:

1 cup all-purpose flour
½ teaspoon baking powder
Dash salt
¼ cup shortening
1 egg
2 Tablespoons water, plus more if necessary

Filling:

8 ounces ground beef
¼ cup minced scallions
2 Tablespoons minced parsley
1 small potato, cooked and mashed
1 medium carrot, cooked, and finely chopped
1½ Tablespoons butter
1 Tablespoon grated Parmesan cheese
Salt and pepper, to taste

To make the dough: combine flour, salt and baking powder in a medium bowl. Cut in shortening with a pastry blender until mixture resembles corn meal. Set aside.

Beat egg; add 2 tablespoons water to egg and mix. Pour the egg mixture into dry ingredients and combine.

If necessary, add additional water a teaspoon at a time until dough holds together. Form dough into a ball, wrap and chill at least 4 hours.

To make meat filling: in a medium frying pan, brown ground beef and onion. Drain fat. Add parsley, potato and carrot and heat through. Add butter, Parmesan, salt and pepper; mix well. Set aside.

To assemble: Roll out the chilled dough on a floured surface to a thickness of about ⅛-inch. Using a bowl or saucer with a diameter of 4 to 5 inches, cut 12 rounds of dough. Place some filling on each dough circle, then fold circle in half to enclose the filling. Dab a little water around the edges of the dough. Using a fork, crimp the edges together to seal.

Prick the tops with a fork to allow steam to escape. Bake the meat pies on greased cookie sheet at 350° for 25 to 30 minutes.

Yield: About 12 meat pasties

Coddled Eggs

This isn't exactly finger food, but coddled eggs make a nice addition to a Sunday brunch tea if you happen to own coddled egg cups or would like to buy some and learn to use them. For variety, substitute smoked salmon for the ham and sprinkle the top with snipped chives.

1 Tablespoon butter
2 slices boiled ham
4 eggs
Salt and pepper

Fill a saucepan about half way with water and set on high heat. Butter the coddled egg cups generously. Cut ham into 1-inch strips, and place around sides and bottom of cups. Break one egg into each cup. Sprinkle with salt and pepper. Put lid on each cup.

Lower heat under saucepan and place cups in simmering water for about 10 minutes, or until set (remove one of the cups and check under lid periodically).

Make sure water level reaches the lids of the egg cups. Unscrew lids and serve eggs with a spoon; or run a spatula around sides of cup to loosen egg and serve in a bowl or on toast.

Yield: 4 servings

Coddled Egg Cups

A coddled egg is a real treat now and then. Similar to a soft-boiled egg, coddled eggs are made in heavy porcelain cups that are usually fitted with metal screw-on lids. The eggs are cracked into the buttered cups, the lids are applied, and then the cups are immersed in simmering water. The lid features a ring on top, which is handy for lifting the hot cups from the water.

Sweets

Currant Scones

Serve these for breakfast or tea, with butter and preserves.

1⅔ cups sifted all-purpose flour
2 teaspoons baking powder
2½ teaspoons sugar
Dash salt
¼ cup butter
2 eggs, beaten (reserve 2 Tablespoons)
5 Tablespoons light cream
½ cup red currants
Granulated sugar, for garnish

In a large bowl, sift together the flour, baking powder, sugar and salt. Cut in the butter with a pastry blender; set aside.

In a small bowl, beat the eggs. Remove 2 tablespoons of the beaten egg and set aside. To the rest of the beaten eggs, add the cream and mix well. Add this mixture and the currants to the dry ingredients, and combine quickly.

Place dough on a floured board. With floured hands, pat down to a thickness of about ¾ inch. Make diagonal cuts halfway through the dough (first one direction then the other) to create diamond-shaped scones.

Place scones on a baking sheet, brush with reserved beaten egg, then sprinkle with granulated sugar. Bake at 400° for 12 to 15 minutes.

Chocolate Chip Scones: substitute ½ cup semisweet chocolate chips for currants in the above recipe.

Parmesan Scones: substitute ½ cup grated Parmesan cheese for the currants in the above recipe. After brushing with beaten egg, sprinkle tops with additional Parmesan.

Yield: About 12 scones

Pecan Shortbread

When scoring the shortbread dough, be sure to cut at least half way through. That way, you'll be able to cut it apart easily after baking.

½ cup pecans
¾ cup butter
6 Tablespoons sugar
½ teaspoon vanilla
1 egg yolk
1¾ cups all-purpose flour
2 Tablespoons cornstarch

Grind pecans to a powder in a food processor; set aside.

In a medium bowl, cream the butter, sugar and vanilla until light. Add egg yolk and mix. Add flour, cornstarch and ground pecans.

Divide dough into two 9-inch pie plates. Press dough flat and smooth top. Crimp outer edge with a fork, pulling dough toward center and away from edge of pie plate.

Score dough into 8 wedges, cutting only halfway through. Plunge tines of fork through each wedge two or three times. Bake at 350° for 25 minutes. Cool on a rack for 15 minutes.

Using a sharp knife, cut along scored lines and separate wedges. Cool completely; store in an airtight container.

Yield: 16 pieces

Raspberry Tea Cookies

If you like, substitute orange marmalade for the raspberry jam or use an assortment of jams and preserves as toppings.

½ cup butter or margarine
6 Tablespoons sugar
2 eggs, separated
1 teaspoon vanilla
½ teaspoon salt
1¼ cups all-purpose flour
½ cup sweetened, flaked coconut
¼ cup raspberry jam

In a medium bowl, cream the butter or margarine with the sugar. Add egg yolks, vanilla and salt. Mix well.

Add flour gradually to the butter mixture and combine well.

Beat egg whites until frothy.

Shape dough into balls and dip into egg white, then roll in coconut. Place on a greased cookie sheet.

Using the back of a teaspoon or your finger, make a well into each ball of dough. Bake at 350° for 15 minutes. Cool on rack. When cool, place a small dollop of jam in the indentation on top of each cookie.

Yield: About 2 dozen cookies

Almond Wafers

Start these the day before you plan to bake them as the dough needs to chill in the refrigerator overnight.

1 cup brown sugar
¼ cup shortening
1 egg
1½ cups all-purpose flour
½ teaspoon baking soda
½ teaspoon salt
½ teaspoon cream of tartar
1 teaspoon almond extract
½ cup almonds, chopped

In a medium bowl, cream brown sugar and shortening until light. Add egg and combine.

Sift flour, baking soda, salt and cream of tartar into sugar mixture and mix. Add almond extract and almonds and combine.

Form the dough into a log about 2 inches high and 4 inches wide, wrap in waxed paper and refrigerate overnight.

To bake, cut dough into ¼-inch slices. Bake on a greased cookie sheet at 350° for 8 to 10 minutes.

Yield: About 2 dozen wafers

Tea on the Run

If you and a friend are meeting for a spot of tea between carpool runs, it is perfectly proper to offer little more than tea plus bread, butter and jam.

Lemon Thins

Make this cookie dough the night before or early in the day, as it needs time to chill in the refrigerator.

1 cup granulated sugar
⅜ cup vegetable shortening
1 egg
1 Tablespoon lemon juice
1 teaspoon freshly grated lemon peel
2 cups all-purpose flour
½ teaspoon salt
½ teaspoon baking soda
½ teaspoon cream of tartar

In a medium bowl combine sugar and shortening until light. Add egg, lemon juice and lemon peel; mix well.

Sift flour, salt, baking soda and cream of tartar into batter, and mix thoroughly.

Form dough into a 2x4 inch log, wrap in waxed paper and chill several hours or overnight.

Slice chilled dough thinly, and bake on an ungreased cookie sheet at 350° for 8 to 10 minutes, or until done.

Yield: About 2 dozen cookies

Cashew Coconut Meringues

For an easy dessert, crush leftover meringues, then layer into parfait glasses with vanilla ice cream and fresh fruit.

3 egg whites
Dash salt
1 cup granulated sugar
½ teaspoon vanilla
1 cup flaked coconut
¼ cup cashews, chopped

In a medium bowl, beat egg whites and salt until almost stiff. Add sugar a little at a time and beat until stiff peaks form.

Fold in the vanilla, coconut and cashews. Drop by rounded teaspoonfuls onto greased cookie sheet.

Bake at 325° for 20 minutes.

Yield: About 24 meringues

Berry Lime Tarts

You can use any berries to garnish these tarts, such as strawberries, blueberries or raspberries.

Crust

¾ cup graham cracker crumbs
2 Tablespoons granulated sugar
½ teaspoon ground cinnamon
¼ cup pecans, finely chopped
¼ cup butter, melted

Filling

3 egg yolks
½ cup granulated sugar
1 teaspoon freshly grated lime peel
1 Tablespoon fresh lime juice
1 Tablespoon water
½ cup whipping cream
1 Tablespoon confectioners' sugar
36 berries for garnish

To make the crust: in a small bowl, combine graham cracker crumbs, sugar, cinnamon and pecans. Add melted butter to the crumb mixture. Stir with a fork to combine.

Coat the wells of a 12-cup muffin tin with vegetable spray. Divide crumb mixture among muffin cups, pressing against bottom and sides with back of a spoon. Bake at 375° for 4 to 5 minutes. Set aside to cool.

To make the filling: in the top of a double boiler, beat egg yolks until light-colored. Add the sugar, lime peel, lime juice and water; mix well. Place over simmering water and cook until very thick. Remove from heat and set aside to cool.

Whip the cream until stiff. Fold in the confectioners' sugar. Fold cooled lime curd into whipping cream. Pour filling into crumb crusts. Chill.

Garnish each tart with a few berries.

Yield: 12 tarts

Banana Pecan Muffins

These are delicious served warm with the Curried Chutney Spread, page 30.

2 cups all-purpose flour
¼ cup sugar
2¼ teaspoons baking powder
¼ teaspoon salt
1 egg, beaten
¾ cup very ripe banana, mashed
⅔ cup milk
3 Tablespoons vegetable oil
½ cup chopped pecans, optional

Grease a 12-cup muffin tin; set aside.

Sift flour, sugar, baking powder and salt together in a medium bowl; set aside.

In another bowl, combine the egg, banana, milk and oil. Add egg mixture and pecans to dry ingredients, mixing until just moist (the batter may be lumpy). Fill each muffin cup two-thirds full.

Bake muffins at 400° for 20 to 25 minutes.

Yield: about 12 muffins

Cleaning a Teakettle

Lime deposits from water build up inside a teakettle. To remove them, mix vinegar and water in equal proportions, fill the kettle, and boil the mixture for 10 minutes. Let cool, swirl mixture around and pour it out. (If the deposits are stubborn, leave the kettle to soak for several hours.) Rinse the kettle out thoroughly. If the kettle has a large opening, you can scrape the bottom with the handle of a wooden spoon or drop in some clean marbles and roll them around to help break up the deposits.

Orange Spice Tea Cake

Cut this cake into little squares to serve.

Cake:

½ cup butter or margarine
1 cup granulated sugar
2 eggs
1 can (6 ounces) frozen orange juice concentrate, thawed
1 teaspoon freshly grated orange peel
⅓ cup milk
¼ cup vegetable oil
2 cups all-purpose flour
½ teaspoon salt
1 teaspoon baking soda
½ teaspoon ground cloves
½ teaspoon ground cinnamon

Glaze:

Reserved orange juice concentrate (3 ounces)
¼ cup chopped walnuts
⅓ cup brown sugar
1 teaspoon cinnamon

Grease and flour a 9x13-inch pan. Set aside.

In a large bowl, cream butter or margarine and granulated sugar until light. Add eggs and mix well.

Add *half* the orange juice concentrate and the orange peel; mix well. Add milk and oil; combine.

Blend the flour, salt, baking soda and spices into creamed mixture; then beat for 2 minutes. Pour batter into a greased and floured 9x13-inch baking pan.

Bake at 350° for 40 to 50 minutes.

Remove from oven and spoon remaining half of orange juice concentrate on top of the warm cake. Combine walnuts, brown sugar and cinnamon. Sprinkle mixture on top of cake. Cool completely.

Yield: 12 to 15 servings

Pineapple Tea Loaf

This tropical style loaf is nice for tea. Toast leftover slices for breakfast the next morning.

½ cup orange juice
2 Tablespoons boiling water
3 Tablespoons vegetable oil
1 egg, beaten
1 cup sugar
2 cups all-purpose flour
½ teaspoon baking powder
1¼ cups dried chopped pineapple
¾ cup chopped pecans or ½ cup sweetened coconut (optional)

In a medium bowl, combine the orange juice, water and oil. Add egg and mix well. Add sugar and mix.

Add flour and baking powder and combine gently until just moist. Fold in pineapple (and nuts or coconut).

Bake in a greased loaf pan at 350° for 50 to 60 minutes, or until done.

Yield: 1 loaf

15-Minute Tea Cakes

These little cakes make a splashy presentation. Use refrigerated, instant or old-fashioned cooked vanilla pudding to ice the cakes, and start with a prepared pound cake from the grocery store.

3-4 Tablespoons clear apple jelly
1 loaf pound cake
1 cup prepared vanilla pudding, chilled
Green seedless grapes, washed and dried
Fresh raspberries, washed and dried
Fresh blueberries, washed and dried
Freshly grated orange peel, for garnish

In a small saucepan, place jelly to melt over low heat.

Cut eight ¾-inch slices of pound cake. Spread cut sides of cake slices with vanilla pudding.

Arrange fruit on top of pudding in a pretty design. Using a brush, carefully glaze the fruit on top of each tea cake with a little warm jelly. Garnish each tea cake with a grating of fresh orange peel. Chill to set the toppings.

Yield: About 8 servings

Cinnamon Bundt Cake

Serve this on your prettiest cake plate, preferably one with a pedestal base.

Topping:

⅓ cup brown sugar
1 teaspoon ground cinnamon

Cake:

2 cups all-purpose flour
1 teaspoon baking soda
1 teaspoon baking powder
Dash salt
1 cup granulated sugar
½ cup butter or margarine
2 eggs
½ cup sour cream
½ cup vegetable oil
1 teaspoon almond extract
½ teaspoon ground cinnamon

To make topping: in a small bowl, combine the brown sugar and ground cinnamon.

To make the cake: grease a Bundt or tube pan; set aside.

In a medium bowl, sift together the flour, baking soda, baking powder and salt; set aside.

In another bowl, cream the sugar and butter until light. Add eggs, and mix well. Add sour cream, oil, almond extract and cinnamon and combine. Beat in dry ingredients until lumps disappear.

Pour half of batter into a greased Bundt or tube pan.

Sprinkle half of topping mixture over batter in baking pan.

Pour rest of batter into pan, and sprinkle on remaining topping mixture. Bake at 350° for 45 to 50 minutes. Cool completely. Gently loosen the cake from the pan by tapping on the bottom or sides of pan. Invert the cake onto a cake plate.

Poppy Seed Cake: omit the almond extract and the brown sugar-cinnamon topping. Measure out ⅓ cup black poppy seeds and soak them in 2 Tablespoons fresh lemon juice for an hour. Make cake batter as directed and add poppy seeds and lemon juice to the batter.

Yield: 12 to 15 servings

Gingerbread with Orange Hard Sauce

Serve this aromatic gingerbread warm with a scoop of chilled Orange Hard Sauce.

Gingerbread:

½ cup butter or margarine
½ cup granulated sugar
1 egg
½ cup light molasses
1¾ cups cake flour
1 teaspoon baking soda
½ teaspoon ground cinnamon
½ teaspoon ground ginger
½ teaspoon black pepper
½ teaspoon salt
½ cup boiling water

Orange Hard Sauce:

4 Tablespoons butter (½ stick), softened
1 cup confectioners' sugar
dash salt
1 teaspoon freshly grated orange rind
2 Tablespoons light cream

To make gingerbread: in a medium bowl, cream butter and sugar until fluffy. Add the egg and molasses and mix well.

In another bowl, sift flour, baking soda, cinnamon, ginger, pepper and salt together. Add dry ingredients alternately with boiling water to egg mixture. Beat well.

Pour into a greased and floured 9-inch square or 7 x 10-inch cake pan. Bake at 350° for about 35 minutes.

To make Orange Hard Sauce: in a small bowl, cream butter, sugar and salt. Add orange rind and mix. Add cream a little at a time and combine. Mixture should be very thick. Refrigerate until thoroughly chilled. To serve, use a mini ice cream scoop to make balls of hard sauce.

Yield: about 8 servings

Strawberry Banana Trifle

The yummy flavors of pound cake, bananas, strawberries and whipped cream blend together wonderfully in this creamy treat.

¾ cup sugar
4 Tablespoons flour
Dash salt
2 cups milk
2 egg yolks, beaten
3 Tablespoons butter
1 teaspoon vanilla
½ of a pound cake, cut into cubes
2 bananas
1 pint fresh strawberries
Sweetened whipped cream for garnish

In a medium saucepan, combine sugar, flour and salt. Add milk and cook on medium heat until thickened, stirring frequently.

Remove from heat. Add 2 tablespoons of the milk mixture to beaten egg yolks and mix, then pour yolks into milk mixture in saucepan. Turn on heat and cook mixture about 2 minutes.

Remove from heat, add butter and vanilla, and mix.

Arrange pound cake on bottom of a trifle dish. Slice bananas and distribute on top of pound cake. Pour pudding over top. Chill several hours.

To serve, place whole strawberries in a ring around the outer rim of trifle dish. Place a generous dollop of sweetened whipped cream in the center of the ring of berries. Spoon trifle onto individual plates.

Yield: About 8 servings

The Color of Brewed Tea

Although tea leaves will lend their color almost immediately after boiling water is added, the flavor and aroma of the tea take a few minutes to fully develop. Don't rush the process and lose the flavor.

Baked Apples and Pears

Serve the fruit in individual dessert bowls. Scrape syrup and bits from bottom of baking pan and distribute over the fruit. Top each serving with a splash of half and half.

3 pears
3 apples
1 cup brown sugar
½ cup walnuts
¼ cup raisins
1 teaspoon ground cinnamon
3 Tablespoons butter, melted
Half and half, as garnish

Wash and core pears and apples; remove a ½-inch ring of peel (exposing the flesh) at the top of each piece of fruit. Place fruit in a decorative buttered baking dish that is just large enough to hold the fruit.

In a small bowl combine the brown sugar, walnuts, raisins and cinnamon. Spoon mixture into hollowed areas of fruit. Drizzle with melted butter.

Bake at 375° for 60 to 70 minutes or until soft.

Yield: 6 servings

Removing Tea Stains from Fabric

As soon as possible, saturate the tea stains with cold water, then rub the spot with detergent. Rinse thoroughly and launder the item as usual. Use chlorine or non-chlorine bleach in the wash cycle as recommended on the item's care label.

Peach Amaretti Syllabub

Crispy amaretti cookies, with their wonderful almond flavor, are found in the cookie section of most grocery stores. To crush the cookies, place them in a plastic bag and roll with a rolling pin.

6 Tablespoons milk
2 Tablespoons almond liqueur
3 Tablespoons confectioners' sugar
1 cup heavy cream
1 package (3 ounces) ladyfingers
3 fresh peaches, peeled, pitted and sliced
1 cup crushed amaretti cookies

Combine milk, almond liqueur and confectioners' sugar in a small bowl.

In a medium bowl, whip cream until peaks form. Beat in the milk mixture a little at a time.

Line the bottom of a souffle dish with ladyfingers. Top with half of the peach slices, and sprinkle with half the amaretti crumbs. Top with cream mixture.

Sprinkle with remaining crumbs, and garnish with reserved peach slices.

Yield: 4 to 5 servings

Caffeine Conscious

Tea contains about half the caffeine of coffee, but you can cut down the caffeine even more by combining traditional tea leaves and herbal leaves for a "half-caff" brew. Or, you may sip decaffeinated teas or straight tisanes for no stimulant effect.

Granita of Tea

Serve this frozen dessert in stemmed dessert cups and garnish each serving with a dollop of whipped cream.

½ cup extra fine granulated sugar
¾ cup (6 ounces) water
4 teaspoons tea leaves
2½ cups (20 ounces) water
½ cup heavy cream
1½ teaspoons confectioners' sugar
½ teaspoon vanilla extract

In a two-quart saucepan over low heat, combine the sugar and water. Stir until the sugar dissolves. Raise the heat and boil 5 minutes. Set aside to cool.

Brew the tea in 2½ cups of water. Strain the tea into the cooled sugar mixture and stir to combine.

Transfer the tea mixture into a five-cup cold-proof container and place in freezer. Stir mixture occasionally. After about 3 hours, the mixture will have a grainy texture and should be ready to serve.

In a small bowl, whip the cream until stiff. Fold in confectioners' sugar and vanilla.

Scoop the granita into individual serving cups and garnish with the flavored whipped cream.

Yield: 5 to 6 servings

Powdered Tea

Powdered tea (not powdered instant tea), by its very consistency, defies the use of a traditional tea strainer. Instead, use a coffee filter when brewing powdered tea.

More About
Tea

The Tea Plant

There are about 3,000 varieties of tea, but they all originate from the *Camellia sinensis* plant, an evergreen bush cultivated in tropical climates. Left to grow in its natural state, the tea plant will grow up to thirty feet high; but on tea estates, the plants are kept pruned to a height of about three to five feet. The pruning results in a denser growth of leaves and is also done for ease of harvesting. Tea bushes like warm temperatures, fertile soil, and plenty of sunshine and rain. The plants are highly adaptable to a variety of terrains. The choicest leaves come from tea grown at higher altitudes (up to 7,000 feet). High-grown teas mature at a slower rate but achieve better flavor and are highly prized.

Teas are named for the areas in which they grow and are known to take on characteristics of the soil they're planted in as well as that of other plants growing adjacent to the tea bushes. For instance, if peach trees are planted among tea bushes, the tea leaves are likely to have a peachy scent. Prominent tea-growing nations include China, India, Sri Lanka (Ceylon), Indonesia, Kenya, Malawi, Tanzania, Taiwan, Japan, Argentina, Brazil, Turkey and the former Soviet Union.

Tea gets its flavor from oils and its astringency and color from tannin. It is a stimulant, but contains only about half as much caffeine as coffee.

Tea Harvest

In some areas, tea bushes flush as often as every week or two. This means the leaves are ready for picking. The rather thick, leathery leaves are picked by hand almost exclusively by women, who pluck off the two newest leaves and one leaf bud from each shoot. The top first and second leaves are considered fine, while the lower leaves are considered coarse.

Tea Processing

There are four classes of finished tea: black, green, oolong and white. The differences among them are attributed to the manner in which the leaves are processed.

Black Tea: The manufacture of black tea involves four stages: withering, rolling, fermentation/oxidization, and drying or firing. Brewed black teas are amber colored, with no bitterness in the taste.

Withering: leaves are spread out in trays to remove their water content, usually through natural evaporation. The process takes about twelve hours.

Rolling: leaves are twisted, spindled and broken up, which causes the cells to seep enzymes onto the surface of the leaves.

Fermentation or Oxidization: the leaves are spread out once again, and the enzymes interact with oxygen for a couple of hours, turning the leaves a coppery color.

Drying or firing: the leaves are placed on trays and exposed to a carefully controlled current of hot air which stops the fermentation process; the leaves turn black.

Green Tea: The manufacture of green tea involves three stages: steaming, rolling, and drying or firing. After being heated in a steamer, the leaves are rolled, then dried or fired. The leaves stay green after this kind of processing, and the tea brewed from these leaves has a raw taste.

Oolong Tea: The manufacture of oolong tea involves three stages: fermentation, rolling, and drying or firing. The leaves are a brownish green after this kind of processing, and the infusion is slightly bitter.

White Tea: The processing for white tea involves only two steps: steaming and drying. White tea is very rare, and its liquor is quite delicate.

Tea Grading and Sorting

After processing, tea is graded and sorted according to style and quality. Quality is determined mainly by brewing the tea and tasting it. Style is a classification of the size and age of the leaves.

Dried black and oolong tea leaves are sifted through large sieves, which results in their being sorted by size into leaf grades and broken grades. There are three leaf grades of tea. From largest to smallest these are: orange pekoe, pekoe and pekoe souchong. Broken grades brew quickly and flavorfully and make up more than three-fourths of all tea leaves. They are designated as: broken orange pekoe, broken pekoe, broken pekoe souchong, fannings and fines (or dust).

Green teas are graded by age of the leaves and by preparation. The three main grades of green teas are:

Gunpowder: consisting of young and medium-aged leaves that are rolled into tight balls.

Imperial: consisting of older gunpowder, with larger, looser leaves.

Hyson: made up of long, twisted leaves; both old and young.

The Romance of Tea

As with most commodities that start out scarce and are withheld from general consumption, tea's value became exaggerated. Thus, tea was bartered and used as money thousands of years ago, and its ingestion was thought to endow the drinker with special vigor and to be intended for higher minds. The struggle for control of tea reaped fortunes but caused much bloodshed.

Before you even take a first sip of hot tea, somehow it's a part of you. The very act of picking up a teacup will result in your pinky finger unfurling like a proud banner. You just "know" that tea is good for you, that tea is restorative. It's all wound up in the notion of tea's link with nature, culture and the power of healing.

Tea has had a practical side, too. Afternoon tea served for a fee to the public has financed the restoration and rebuilding of ancient castles. The cargo of sunken ships has revealed crates of pristine chinaware whose finish seems to have been preserved against the ravages of seawater by the loose tea that cushioned its long-ago journey from Asia to the west.

Literature teems with references to the delights of taking tea. Even the English language is peppered with tea terms: You may have attended a tea dance or been entertained at a tearoom, and you probably have declared, at least once in your life, "It's not my cup of tea."

The Mystique: Reading Tea Leaves

Geomancy is a kind of fortune-telling that assumes a connection between the natural world and human beings. It involves the examination of the stars, dirt, the palm of the hand or tea leaves to read the observable patterns in search of hidden meanings that reveal the future.

The first requirement for reading tea leaves is a cup of tea made with loose leaves. Tea bags simply don't lend themselves to the process. In reading tea leaves, the teacup is inverted, turned several times, then tapped on the base; or, the cup is swirled a couple of times and then turned upside down on the saucer.

The reader picks up the cup to see how the tea leaves are distributed. Each part of the cup (the rim, the base, the handle, etc.) as well as the pattern of the leaves is considered significant. For example, a chain pattern might suggest a trip while a circle can mean marriage. Leaves clinging near the cup's handle relate to events in the home, but leaves clustered at the bottom of the cup foretell happenings in the distant future.

The patterns formed and the location of the patterns in the cup are meaningful. Thus, a circle pattern in the base of the cup is thought to predict a future marriage; and a chain of leaves around the rim of the cup might symbolize a trip to be taken right away. With a little practice and imagination you can regale your guests with your tea- leaf reading ability.

The Legend and the Reality

For thousands of years teas and tisanes have been the basis for mystery, superstition and folk remedies. Witch doctors, shamans and herbalists collected plants and dispensed the brews of healing. Tea was thought to aid digestion and concentration, and to stimulate. Tea was taken as a purgative or a decongestant and applied as a healing lotion.

Abyssinian tea, really a tisane, seems to have been a narcotic stimulant. Breast tea, pertaining to the chest, was a household remedy for respiratory disorders prepared from cut and bruised althaea, coltsfoot, licorice root, anise, mullein flowers and orrisroot. The ingestion of hops or valerian herb tea had a quieting effect. Eyestrain was relieved by the application of wet tea bags and bad breath covered up by sipping peppermint tea.

It's hard to know where the lore stops and reality begins, but there is logic in some of the health applications of tea. The tannin in tea is an astringent, a property that shrinks tissues. So, when your dentist suggests applying a wet tea bag to the site of an extracted tooth, or a friend recommends hot tea with lemon and honey to soothe a sore throat, there is something to the idea that your condition will improve if you do so.

Other beneficial aspects of tea consumption are that the ingestion of fluid is therapeutic, that boiled water is healthier (especially so in some parts of the world) and that the water itself may contain fluoride. There is also a lot of vitamin C in green tea and several B complex vitamins can be found in other teas. Recent medical studies have shown that tea *might* inhibit the growth of certain cancerous tumors as well as aid in the prevention of heart disease and in lowering cholesterol.

Plain tea contains no fat, sodium, sugar, additives, preservatives, artificial colors, artificial flavors or calories and its manufacture is an all-natural process.

Herb Teas or Tisanes

Tea can be made out of anything edible. Steeping leaves, berries, spices, herbs or vegetables in boiling water yields "tea." Indeed, these kinds of infusions or tisanes, as they are more appropriately called, were central to the beginnings of curative medicine thousands of years ago. Some of the primitive brews were much later found to be truly effective such as the digitalis that came from foxglove or the infusion made from willow bark that turned out to be aspirin.

Some herb teas have a soothing, almost sedative effect. Others seem to clear the sinuses, reduce foot odor, alleviate hives or relieve the symptoms of gout. Today, herb teas are enjoying great popularity. Sipping an herbal brew at breakfast or after a meal is relaxing and provides a feeling of well-being. They do not contain caffeine, are warm and aromatic and offer at least the hope that you are doing something kind, perhaps even healthy, for yourself.

The following are some of the most common herbs, seeds and blossoms used in infusions and decoctions, either alone or in combination. They are also used to flavor and enhance traditional tea brews. Generally speaking, they are prepared by two methods: infusion, which is done by steeping leaves and blossoms in boiling water for a few minutes; and decoction, which involves boiling hard substances like bark, seeds or roots for one-half hour to an hour or more.

Anise: an aromatic herb of the carrot family. The seeds are used for flavoring, the oil is used for flavor and fragrance and the leaves are used for seasoning and garnishing. It was once used to clear sinuses.

Balm: an aromatic perennial herb from the mint family with lemon-scented leaves that were once thought to be effective in controlling nausea.

Barley: a cereal grass cultivated since prehistoric times, barley water was once used for its mildly medicinal value and is now used to flavor malt beverages and in breakfast food.

Bergamot: a small tree with lemon-yellow fruits that yield a fragrant oil used also for flavor.

Cardamom: an herb cultivated for its seeds and used as a spice, thought to have stimulant and purgative qualities.

Catnip: an aromatic herb once used to make catnip tea, thought to relieve colic and colds.

Chamomile: this herb of the daisy family cultivated for its aromatic foliage and stems was thought to be good for many physical complaints such as hives and sore throat because of its sedative property.

Clove: a tropical evergreen whose dried flower buds are cultivated as a spice.

Fenugreek: an asiatic herb with aromatic seeds used to flavor foods and as a decongestant.

Ginseng: herbaceous plants whose fleshy roots are considered a valuable and effective medicine by the Chinese.

Hop: a climbing vine of Eurasia, its flowers feature yellow, dust-like bitter grains that are used as a flavoring and were considered to have a sedative effect.

Jasmine: shrubs whose fragrant flowers are dried and added to tea.

Labrador: an evergreen of eastern North America sometimes used to make a tea.

Lemongrass: a grass with a lemony scent grown in India and cultivated as a source of lemongrass oil flavoring.

Licorice: a herbaceous plant with fibrous roots from which comes a sweet black extract. It is used as a flavoring and was thought to be an anesthetic agent.

Maté: South American evergreen shrub of the holly family whose prickly leaves contain caffeine and are used to brew yerba maté or Paraguay tea.

Mint: an aromatic herb whose leaves are used fresh or dried to flavor foods, and whose strong oil lends fragrance to perfumes and soaps. It has been used to combat foot odor, bad breath and gout.

Oswego tea: a North American mint called bee balm.

Paraguay tea: see Maté.

Passionflower: a tropical climbing vine with large berries whose pulp is used to flavor beverages and was considered effective against hives.

Raspberry leaf: a member of the rose family.

Rosehip: the edible fruit of a rose which is dried and used to flavor tea.

Sage: herbaceous and shrubby plant with aromatic leaves that are dried and used to flavor foods, but once was brewed as a tea and served as a tonic.

Sarsaparilla: a plant whose dried roots are decocted and used as a flavoring.

Sassafras: from the laurel family, the aromatic bark of the roots is used to make tea and to flavor other foods.

Thyme: from the mint family, whose leaves are dried and ground and used as seasoning but formerly was used medicinally for fever.

Valerian: an herb whose aromatic roots and underground stems are dried and used to make a tea thought to have a sedative effect.

Yarrow: an herbaceous perennial of the daisy family whose aromatic leaves are used to make a tea; once considered helpful to gout sufferers.

Glossary of Teas & Tea Terms

The trade names of teas appear in capital letters.

Afternoon tea: a social occasion where a light snack is served at tea-time, composed of finger sandwiches, sweets and hot tea. See also *High tea.*

ASSAM: a black tea from northeastern India.

Astringent: a taste characteristic of tea or a substance that shrinks the tissues of the body. Tannin, found in tea, has astringent or drying properties.

BANCHA: a Japanese green tea of lesser quality that is made from stalks and roasted.

BLACK DRAGON: an oolong tea grown in China and Taiwan.

Black tea: the class of tea most widely distributed; grown mostly in China and India.

Blend: a combination of two or more teas that results in an altered flavor, complexity and character than the original ingredients possess individually; a blend can also feature the addition of blossoms and herbs.

Brack: an Irish cake or loaf containing seeds or fruit.

Brick tea: compressed cakes of tea leaf bits once used as currency as well as to brew tea during China's Tang dynasty, A.D. 618-906.

Broken leaf tea: a grade of processed black tea leaves comprising (from largest to smallest) broken orange pekoe, broken pekoe, broken pekoe souchong, fannings, and dust.

Caddy spoon: a one-teaspoon measuring utensil for tea leaves that is usually stored in a tea caddy.

Camellia sinensis: the tea plant from which all teas originate.

CEYLON: see *Sri Lanka.*

CHINA CARAVAN: a blend of black Keemun teas from China.

CHINA WHITE: a rare white tea from China.

CHINESE RESTAURANT: a blend of oolong and green teas.

CHIN MEE: a green tea produced in Taiwan.

Class: a system of classifying tea according to its manner of manufacture or processing. Classes of tea are black, green, oolong and white.

Congou: a whole-leaf grade of black tea from China, constituted of lower leaves of the plant.

DARJEELING: a large-leaf black tea grown in the Himalayas of India which is considered the champagne of teas.

Decoction: a liquid preparation made by boiling a plant or bark in water, thereby extracting its flavor.

DRAGON WELL: a fine green tea grown in China.

Drying: firing, which is the last step in the processing of black, green and white tea, stops the fermentation process, seals in the flavor and oil and preserves the tea leaves.

Dust: tiny tea leaf particles, also called fines, which is the smallest broken-leaf grade of tea. It brews very quickly and is often used in tea bags.

Earl Grey: a scented black tea blend of China tea flavored with oil of bergamot.

English Breakfast: a black tea blend composed of Keemun or Assam and Sri Lanka (Ceylon) tea.

Fanciest Formosa: an oolong tea from Taiwan.

Fannings: a broken-leaf grade of tea; coarse tea siftings that result after the manufacture of tea.

Fermentation (oxidation): a step in the processing of black and oolong tea where the tea juices and enzymes produced by rolling are exposed to the air. This results in changes of color from green to copper and aroma, from leafy to fruity.

FLOWERY WHITE PEKOE: a rare white tea from China.

Flush: the harvest of tea leaves; the first flush is considered very high in quality.

FORMOSA OOLONG: an oolong tea from Taiwan, considered to be the best oolong in the world.

FORMOSA POUCHONG: an oolong tea from Taiwan that is blended with dried blossoms such as jasmine and gardenia.

GEORGIAN: tea grown in the Georgian Republic, formerly part of the U.S.S.R.

Grade: a method of rating tea leaves, with the smallest leaf receiving the highest grade. Congou, pekoe, orange pekoe and souchong are the grades and each grade is further marked by when the leaves were picked, with No. 1 meaning the first harvest.

Green tea: a class of tea grown predominantly in China and Japan with delicate flavor; graded by age of leaves and preparation.

GUNPOWDER: a grade of green tea that is rolled into tiny balls that unfurl "explosively" when boiling water is added. It is made of young and semi-young leaves. It is also a trade name.

GYOKURO: the finest green tea from Japan.

Harvest: see *Flush.*

Herbal tea or tisane: an infusion of leaves, blossoms, seeds, bark or berries of plants other than the *Camellia sinensis* in water.

High tea: a meal in the late afternoon; composed of a main course entrée, salad and such, served with hot tea. (See also *Afternoon tea.*)

HOOCHOW: a green tea from China.

Hyson: a grade of Chinese green tea with long leaves of varying ages.

Iced tea: a cold beverage created during the 1904 Louisiana Purchase Exposition in St. Louis, Missouri.

Imperial: a grade of green tea with older, larger leaves.

Infusion: the extract that results from steeping or soaking a substance or plant in water.

IRISH BREAKFAST: a blend of African black teas.

IRON GODDESS OF MERCY: an oolong tea.

JASMINE: a blend of green China tea scented with dried jasmine blossoms.

KEEMUN: a black tea grown in Hao Ya Mountains in China; used in English Breakfast tea.

KENYA: a black, high-grown tea from Africa.

LAPSANG SOUCHONG: a black tea from China with a smoky, strong flavor.

Leaf tea: a grade of processed black tea leaves such as orange pekoe, pekoe and pekoe souchong.

LUNG CHING: a green tea from China.

MATCHA: a powdered green tea, served during the Japanese tea ceremony according to strict ritual.

Mote spoon: a utensil for removing undesirable particles like tea leaves from poured cups of tea.

NILIGRI: a black, high-grown tea from southern India.

NORTH CHINA: a black-leaf Congou tea produced in China.

Oolong: a class of tea grown mostly in China and Taiwan.

Orange pekoe: the name of a whole-leaf grade of black tea, whose leaves are long and twisted; "orange" does not refer to the color but to the House of Orange, a royal family in Europe that ruled in the United Kingdom from 1688 to 1694 and in the Netherlands since 1815, under whose rule and in whose name tea estates were sponsored around the world.

PAKLUM: a black tea from China.

Pekoe: (pronounced peck-o) is a Chinese word for leaf. It is the name of a leaf grade of black tea whose leaves are small and curled.

Pekoe tip: the name of a whole-leaf grade of black tea, this is the term for the first and second leaves on a shoot of tea. The "tips" are top-quality fuzzy leaf buds that are often rolled, curled and twisted by hand.

PI LO CHUN: a green tea that is rolled into spring-like forms. It has a fine, fruity aroma.

PINGSUENG: a very fine green tea from China.

Plucking: the harvesting of tea leaves, which is usually done by women and almost always by hand.

Rolling: a step in the processing of black, green and oolong teas that turns, curls and breaks the leaves, causing juices and enzymes to emerge on the surface of the leaves.

ROSE POUCHONG: a black tea from China blended with dried rose petals.

RUSSIAN: a blend of Keemun and Assam black teas with Chinese green tea.

Sachet: a tea bag filter packet that holds dried tea leaves and flavorings for brewing; a tea bag. Thomas Sullivan, a New York tea merchant is credited with inventing the tea bag in the early 1900s.

SENCHA: a green tea from Japan.

Souchong: the name of a leaf grade of black tea, whose leaves are large and take longer to brew.

SOUTH CHINA: a red leaf congou variety of black tea produced in China.

SOW MEE: a green tea produced in Taiwan.

SRI LANKA: previously called **Ceylon**, it is a black, best-quality tea.

Steep: to infuse or soak in hot liquid in order to extract flavor.

Tablet tea: tea dust that is pressed into tablet form and used to brew a single cup of tea.

Tannin: an alkaloid substance with a bitter taste found in tea and some tree barks; tannin gives tea its astringency and color.

Tea ball: a hollow, perforated ball designed to hold loose tea during the brewing process; a type of infuser.

Tea bell: a bell rung to announce tea time.

Tea biscuit: a small, round, soft biscuit, usually sweet.

Tea boiler: a vessel used to boil water; a teakettle.

Tea board: a tray to hold a tea set and accessories.

Tea bowl: a tea cup without a handle.

Tea bread: bread or buns served with tea.

Tea caddy: a small, compartmentalized box, tin or chest for storing tea leaves.

Tea cake: a light, flat cake.

Tea cart: a serving tray on wheels.

Tea case: a case that holds small articles (like spoons) used at teatime.

Tea clipper: a fast-sailing ship formerly used in the tea trade.

Tea cloth: a small tablecloth.

Tea coat: a garment worn by women at the tea table.

Tea cooper: a dock worker who unloads tea and repairs crates.

Tea cozy: an insulated cloth teapot cover.

Tea dance: a late afternoon social event where tea is served and dancing takes place.

Tea dish: former name for a teacup.

Tea estate: a plantation where tea is cultivated.

Tea hound: someone very fond of tea, a habitué.

Teahouse: a restaurant where tea and refreshments are served.

Teakettle: a portable kettle with a cover, spout, and handle.

Tea maker: a perforated covered spoon that holds tea for brewing one cup.

Tea ring: a yeast coffee cake.

Tea roller: a machine for rolling or curling tea leaves.

Tearoom: a restaurant that specializes in serving tea and refreshments.

Tea set: tea-serving equipment, composed of a kettle, teapot, waste bowl, extra pouring pot, sugar bowl, milk pitcher and a tray.

Tea sifter: an apparatus used to sift processed tea leaves.

Tea taster: a person whose profession it is to taste and grade tea.

Teatime: traditionally 4 p.m., but also refers to the dinner or supper hour.

Tea tongs: former name for sugar tongs.

Tea urn: a footed urn with a tiny faucet that is used as a hot water supply in brewing tea for large groups of people.

Tea wine: a fermented liquor made from tea.

TENCHA: a green tea from Japan.

Tidbit tray: see Handled hostess tray.

Tisane: an herbal beverage. It was originally an infusion of barley and water but now of dried leaves, blossoms, seeds, bark or berries and water. Historically thought to have medicinal properties.

Trifle: a dessert of cake and fruit topped with custard or cream.

White tea: a rare class of tea from China; processing of its leaves involves only steaming and drying.

Withering: the first step in the manufacture of black tea.

YIN CHEN: a rare white tea produced in China.

YIN HAO JASMINE: the finest quality green tea and jasmine blend. It is grown in China and is noted as James Bond's tea of choice.

YUNNAN: a black tea from western China.

Supplementary Reading List

Afternoon Tea Delicacies, Young, Grace. Copyright 1993. Bantam Doubleday Dell, 1540 Broadway, New York, NY 10036. ISBN: 0-385-42586-4.

All the Tea in China, Chow, Kit and Kramer, Ione. Copyright 1990. China Books and Periodicals, Inc., 2929 - 24th Street, San Francisco, CA 94110. ISBN: 0-8351-2194-1.

The Book of Tea, Burgess, Anthony. Copyright 1993. Abbeville Press, 488 Madison Avenue, New York, NY 10022. ISBN: 0-208013-533-3.

Coffee and Tea, McCoy, Elin and Walker, John F. Copyright 1991. Thero Raines, Raines & Raines, 71 Park Avenue, New York, NY 10016.

A Decent Cup of Tea, McCormick, Malachi. Copyright 1991. Clarkson N. Potter, Inc., 2901 East 50th Street, New York, NY 10022. ISBN: 0-517-58462-X.

Tea Rooms & Tea Service, Printed in three volumes, Giordano, Karen. Copyright 1994. Mary Mac's Press, P. O. Box 841, Langley, WA 98260.

Tea-Time at the Inn, Greco, Gail. Copyright 1991. Rutledge Hill Press, Nashville, TN. ISBN: 1-55853-120-3.